Sales 2.0

Mastering Technology to Boost Revenue and Stay Ahead

Taylor Royce

DEDICATION

To all of the inventors, leaders, and salespeople who are always pushing the envelope of what is conceivable. The real change agents in this always changing industry are your dedication to expansion, your pursuit of quality, and your readiness to adopt new technologies.

This book is devoted to people who aren't satisfied with simply hitting goals but are committed to transforming sales through the use of innovation, technology, and a forward-thinking approach in order to achieve long-term success. I hope that this exploration of sales technology will motivate you to not only adjust but also prosper in the sales industry of the future.

This is for the pioneers, the visionaries, and the doers.

DISCLAIMER

This book's content is intended solely for general informative purposes. Although every attempt has been taken to guarantee the content's accuracy and dependability, the author and publisher make no guarantees or assurances about the information's completeness, accuracy, or applicability.

Before making any judgments or putting any methods based on the information in this book into practice, the reader is encouraged to do their own study and speak with pertinent professionals or experts in the field. Any mistakes, omissions, or losses resulting from the use or reliance on the information provided are not the responsibility of the author or publisher.

The thoughts contained in this book are those of the author and may not represent the views or stances of any organizations or entities mentioned. It is not meant to be a source of legal or professional advice.

By reading this book, you consent to indemnify the

publisher, author, and any related parties for any losses, damages, or claims arising from the use or interpretation of the information contained within.

CONTENTS

ACKNOWLEDGMENTS

My heartfelt appreciation goes out to all those who helped make this book possible. This adventure would not have been possible without your encouragement, support, and wisdom.

Above all, I want to express my sincere gratitude to my family and friends for their unfailing support and believe in me during the writing process. I couldn't have done this without your love and understanding, which served as my compass.

I would especially like to express my gratitude to the salespeople, business executives, and specialists who so kindly shared their expertise with me. Your practical knowledge and experience served as a great source of inspiration and influenced the book's content.

I am grateful to my mentors and colleagues who have helped shape my understanding of technology and sales throughout my career. Your insight has consistently served as a source of motivation.

Lastly, I would like to express my sincere gratitude to all of the readers, regardless of your level of experience in sales. Your interest and drive for excellence in the field of sales technology inspire me to keep sharing my knowledge. I believe this book will be a useful tool to guide you through and help you succeed in the dynamic world of contemporary sales.

We appreciate everyone's belief in and support of this work.

CHAPTER 1

TECHNOLOGY AND SALES WORK TOGETHER

1.1 How Sales Change in a Technological Age

Sales has changed dramatically, moving from a relationship-based, time-consuming process to one that makes use of the speed and accuracy of contemporary technology. There are three main stages to this evolution:

- **Customary Sales:** Face-to-face interactions and human rapport were key components of most sales. These included telephone marketing, in-store promotions, and door-to-door sales, where the salesperson's charm and ability to persuade were crucial.

- **The Digital Transition:** E-commerce and online marketplaces were made possible by the development of the internet, which allowed companies to access customers around the world. Sales methods now heavily rely on tools like social media, email advertising, and simple customer databases.

- **The hybrid model is as follows:** We observe a combination of technology technologies and human knowledge today. Sales teams can provide individualized experiences at scale thanks to automation, artificial intelligence (AI), and customer relationship management (CRM) tools. Sales are now experiential rather than transactional, with an emphasis on establishing credibility and adding value over time.

This development represents a fundamental shift in how companies view and engage with their clientele, not just a change in approach. Instead of taking the role of the human element, technology has improved it by enabling more strategic, data-driven decision-making.

1.2 Technology's Place in Contemporary Sales

Technology is now the foundation of successful sales tactics in the digital age. It helps companies to develop enduring relationships and loyalty by going beyond simple transactions. Technology plays important roles in sales, including:

- **Collection and Analysis of Data:** Customer data is gathered and analyzed by tools such as CRMs, which offer insights into preferences, behaviors, and buying trends. Sales teams can use this information to customize their strategies for optimal effect.

- **Automation of Typical Activities:** Data entry, email follow-ups, and lead generation are examples of repetitive tasks that technology manages. This enables salespeople to concentrate on high-value tasks like customer interaction and strategy.

- **Improved Customer Engagement:** AI-driven chatbots, tailored marketing emails, and recommendation engines enable ongoing, significant communication with clients. By making clients feel appreciated, these methods improve retention rates.

- **Forecasting & Predictive Analytics:** To forecast client requirements and sales results, sophisticated AI technologies examine past data and market patterns. By foreseeing desires before they materialize, this helps businesses stay ahead of the competition.

The ability to maintain consistent branding and messaging across several channels, including social media, websites, physical stores, and mobile apps, is made possible by technology.

Higher conversion rates and long-term growth are made possible by the more effective, responsive, and customer-focused approach that technology integration in sales fosters.

1.3 Why the Pandemic Hastened the Uptake of Technology

Technology adoption in a variety of industries, including sales, was accelerated by the COVID-19 pandemic. Due to supply chain disruptions, social alienation, and lockdowns, companies had to fast adapt in order to survive.

- The transition to virtual sales Businesses switched to virtual platforms like Zoom, Microsoft Teams, and Slack for client meetings, presentations, and negotiations as in-person interactions proved impractical. Conventional in-person events were supplanted by webinars and virtual product demos.

- **The boom in e-commerce:** Due to the closure of physical stores, companies made significant investments in e-commerce platforms. In addition to giving them a lifeline during the pandemic, this allowed them to reach unexplored markets.

- **More Investing in Automation and CRM:** CRM systems were used by businesses to remotely manage their customer interactions. In order to handle the rise in online questions and guarantee prompt responses, automation techniques became crucial.

- **AI-Powered Perspectives:** An unparalleled degree of unpredictability was brought about by the pandemic. Businesses used AI tools to monitor new patterns, changes in consumer behavior, and market developments in real time.

- **Emphasis on Empathy for Customers:** Technology made it possible for companies to take a more sympathetic stance. Technology enabled businesses to sensitively respond to client needs, from flexible payment choices to targeted communications addressing pandemic-related concerns.

This quick adoption of technology was a game-changer rather than merely a band-aid fix. Companies that used these technologies during the epidemic are still reaping the benefits of increased customer happiness, agility, and efficiency.

The combination of technology and sales has completely changed the market, allowing companies to prosper in a world that is driven by customers and moves quickly. This chapter emphasizes the continuous development, the critical function of technology, and the pandemic's revolutionary influence on contemporary sales techniques.

CHAPTER 2

Technology's Advantages for Sales

2.1 Increasing Productivity

Productivity is frequently the primary factor that separates success from stagnation in the fast-paced world of sales. Sales teams now work differently because of technology, which streamlines processes, automates tedious duties, and allows for greater strategic focus.

Among the main ways that technology increases productivity are:

Repetitive Task Automation:
Manual processes like arranging follow-ups, entering data, and prioritizing leads are eliminated by tools like calendar integrations, lead scoring systems, and email automation software. For instance, CRM systems update client profiles in real-time, and automated email campaigns may nurture

prospects at scale.

Simplified Inventory Control:

Inventory management systems give companies that deal with tangible goods real-time stock level updates, which lowers errors and guarantees sales teams have precise product availability. Delays are avoided, and consumer trust is increased.

Team members may access critical information at any time and from any location thanks to cloud-based CRMs and sales platforms. For remote or hybrid sales teams, this flexibility is especially crucial for maintaining team alignment.

The sales, marketing, and customer care teams can communicate and work together more easily thanks to tools like Slack, Microsoft Teams, and project management systems. Better lead conversion and customer retention are guaranteed with a more integrated strategy.

Sales teams may spend more time on high-value tasks like relationship development, strategy planning, and deal closing by optimizing processes. Better performance and increased team spirit result from this.

2.2 Improving Knowledge of Customers

Understanding the customer is essential to successful sales. Technology has completely changed how companies collect and analyze data, allowing for a more thorough understanding of the wants, needs, and problems of their customers.

Technology has made significant advances to our understanding of customers, including:

Buyer Personas and Data Analytics:
To create thorough buyer personas, tools like HubSpot, Salesforce, and Google Analytics gather and examine consumer data. Through the identification of demographics, hobbies, and purchasing patterns, these personas direct sales techniques.

Monitoring Consumer Behavior:
Businesses are able to track how customers use their digital

platforms thanks to technologies like clickstream data, website cookies, and heatmaps. This data shows which goods or services are most desirable and where clients may run into problems during the sales process.

Personalized Marketing Campaigns: AI-powered technologies allow for extremely tailored communications. For example:

- Dynamic emails are automated messages that are customized based on user preferences.
- Recommendation engines make product recommendations based on browsing or previous purchases.
- Businesses can proactively address future client requirements and behaviors by using predictive analytics.

Emotional Evaluation:

Businesses may measure customer happiness and modify their tactics by utilizing AI to evaluate feedback forms, social media comments, and customer reviews.

By making consumers feel appreciated and understood,

improving customer comprehension not only increases sales but also cultivates enduring loyalty.

2.3 Boosting Sales Increase

Increasing revenue is the ultimate objective of incorporating technology into sales. Businesses can reach more clients, close sales more quickly, and create enduring relationships with the help of cutting-edge tools and platforms.

Among the main ways that technology boosts sales are:

- **Conversational AI:** Voice assistants and chatbots have revolutionized consumer interactions by offering prompt answers to questions, helping customers choose products, and providing troubleshooting assistance. Among the examples are:
- Available around-the-clock, chatbots interact with clients in real time, addressing problems and providing answers to frequently asked questions without the need for human assistance.
- **Voice Assistants:** Programs such as Google

Assistant and Alexa streamline ordering procedures and offer prompt product recommendations.

Lead Nurturing and Conversion: Technology makes sure that prospective clients are constantly exposed to pertinent information by automating the lead nurturing process. Sites such as Pardot and Marketo offer:

- Sequentially distributed material that informs and convinces leads is known as a drip campaign.
- In order to assist sales teams in concentrating on the most potential prospects, Lead Scoring: assigns scores based on lead behavior.

Cross-selling and Upselling:

Customers are encouraged to investigate higher-value or complementary products by AI-driven recommendations. An e-commerce platform might, for instance, advertise premium upgrades or recommend accessories for a purchased item.

The checkout process is made simpler with integrated payment systems like PayPal or Stripe, which lower cart abandonment rates and boost conversion.

International Presence Via Digital Platforms:

Geographical boundaries are broken by technology, which enables companies to access a wider audience. Localized websites, social media advertisements, and e-commerce platforms allow businesses to reach clients all over the world.

Businesses can increase revenue and develop a scalable, sustainable development model by utilizing these strategies.

Revenue generation, customer interaction, and productivity have all been changed by the use of technology in sales. Technology enables sales teams to work at their highest level by automating repetitive processes, offering insightful data, and fostering creative customer interactions. The advantages of technology in sales will only increase as companies continue to embrace digital transformation, guaranteeing long-term success and a competitive edge.

CHAPTER 3

SALES AND ARTIFICIAL INTELLIGENCE

3.1 The Function of AI in Customization

Successful sales techniques now rely heavily on personalization, and artificial intelligence is leading the way in allowing companies to establish individualized connections with their clients. AI-powered hyper-personalized approaches are replacing traditional segmentation techniques based on broad categories like demographics or past purchases.

The following are important facets of AI's role in personalization:

Scale Data Analysis:
Large volumes of consumer data are processed by AI systems, including browsing patterns, social media activity, past purchases, and even sentiment analysis from reviews

and comments. This makes it possible to fully comprehend the preferences and problems of every client.

Dynamic Content Creation: AI-driven technologies are able to produce customized offers in email campaigns or product recommendations on e-commerce platforms. For instance:

- The "You might also like" sections in e-commerce are based on each user's browsing history.
- **Email Marketing:** Tailored content and subject lines based on the interests of the recipient.

Personalized in Real Time:

During client involvement, AI makes sure that interactions change dynamically. Chatbots, for example, can modify their answers according to the customer's tone, level of urgency, or past questions.

Mapping the Customer Journey:

AI determines the best touchpoints to engage clients by examining interaction data, guaranteeing prompt interventions that advance them through the sales funnel.

Because they feel heard and appreciated, clients who receive this degree of personalization are more engaged and loyal. Personalized experiences dramatically boost conversion rates and lifelong customer value, according to numerous studies.

3.2 Predictive analytics and automation

The productivity and efficacy of sales teams have been revolutionized by AI's capacity to automate repetitive work and forecast future trends. Businesses can function more strategically and proactively because of this twin ability of automation and foresight.

Among AI's major achievements in this field are:

Automation of Sales Activities:
- **Email Campaigns:** AI automated drip campaigns, nurturing leads with the appropriate message at the appropriate moment.
- In order to ensure that sales teams concentrate on the most potential leads, artificial intelligence (AI) technologies such as HubSpot or Salesforce Einstein

assess leads according to predetermined criteria.

- **Follow-Up Reminders:** AI-driven systems make sure no opportunity is lost by scheduling timely reminders for sales teams.

Predictive Analytics for Strategic Planning: AI forecasts consumer behavior and sales results by utilizing market trends and previous data. Among the examples are:

- Predicting the long-term worth of a client connection in order to give priority to high-value leads is known as customer lifetime value, or CLV.
- Demand forecasting is the process of predicting the demand for a product or service by taking into account variables including consumer preferences, market conditions, and seasonality.
- Possibilities for upselling and cross-selling include spotting trends in consumer purchasing to recommend premium or related goods.

Marketing Funnel Optimization:

Businesses can boost conversion rates and optimize their strategy by using predictive analytics to find bottlenecks in the sales funnel.

AI allows sales teams to concentrate on establishing connections and closing deals by automating repetitive operations and providing actionable insights, which eventually leads to increased productivity and profitability.

3.3 Virtual assistants and conversational AI

Conversational AI's development has completely changed how companies communicate with their clientele. Natural language processing (NLP) and machine learning-driven chatbots and virtual assistants offer scalable, effective, and human-like interaction across several touchpoints.

Conversational AI in sales has several important features and advantages, such as:

Availability: 24/7:
Regardless of time zones or business hours, virtual assistants guarantee that client inquiries are answered promptly. This accessibility speeds up reaction times and improves client satisfaction.

Adaptive and Natural Interactions:

Conversational AI solutions can now recognize sentiment, comprehend context, and react properly thanks to developments in natural language processing. Customers feel heard and understood as a result of more human-like interactions.

Scalability: Conversational AI allows companies to manage several interactions at once. Chatbots are scalable without sacrificing quality, whether they are handling hundreds of website visitors or answering questions on social media.

Qualification and Lead Generation: AI-powered chatbots interact with website users, pose qualifying queries, and forward high-potential leads to human sales agents. For example:

- To determine purpose, a chatbot may inquire, "What specific product are you interested in?"
- It assigns a lead score and arranges a call with a salesman based on the responses.

Effective Integration with Additional Tools:

Virtual assistants deliver contextually relevant information by integrating with knowledge bases, email platforms, and CRMs. For instance, the chatbot can rapidly deliver a status update and pull information from the CRM if a consumer asks about an order.

Efficiency in Cost:

Businesses free up human employees to work on more complex or valuable activities by automating regular customer care interactions.

Real-World Uses:

- **E-commerce:** AI chatbots, such as those employed by Amazon or Alibaba, respond to millions of consumer inquiries every day by offering suggestions and fixing problems.
- **Banking:** Bank of America's virtual assistants, such as Erica, aid clients in tracking their spending, managing their accounts, and creating financial objectives.
- **Retail:** AI-powered chatbots and kiosks help shoppers online and in-store with product recommendations and questions.

Conversational AI, which combines effectiveness with a human touch, is a huge advancement in customer engagement. By ensuring regular, timely communication, it not only improves the client experience but also increases sales.

AI has emerged as a crucial tool in contemporary sales, allowing companies to automate processes, customize interactions, and accurately forecast client wants. The uses of AI are numerous and revolutionary, ranging from developing highly focused advertising campaigns to using conversational AI to provide scalable customer service. Businesses that use AI will stay ahead of the competition as technology develops further, spurring expansion and creating long-lasting client relationships.

CHAPTER 4

DEVELOPMENTS IN CUSTOMER RELATIONSHIP MANAGEMENT (CRM)

Systems for managing customer relationships (CRM) have become essential tools for companies looking to improve customer interaction, optimize processes, and cultivate enduring loyalty. This chapter explores the revolutionary developments in CRM technology and how they will affect customer relations going forward.

4.1 The Development of All-Inclusive CRMs

CRMs' conventional function as contact databases has greatly grown. Contemporary CRMs are dynamic, all-inclusive platforms that combine several facets of corporate operations and consumer engagement into a single, cohesive system.

Important developments include:

Management of Multi-Channel Communication:

CRMs today facilitate smooth communication via social media, chat, phone, email, and more. Companies can respond to consumer issues and keep up regular communication on the channels of their choice. For instance, a client who tweets about a problem can have it addressed and followed up with via email without losing context.

Mapping the Customer Journey:

From first interaction to conversion and beyond, advanced CRMs offer comprehensive customer path visualizations. Businesses can use this to pinpoint problems and improve their engagement tactics.

Centralized Information Gathering and Access:

Every piece of consumer information, including demographics and purchase patterns, is kept in one place. This eliminates silos and enhances teamwork by guaranteeing that the marketing, sales, and customer support departments have access to the same current data.

Complementary System Integration:

In order to create a unified digital ecosystem, comprehensive CRMs interface with marketing tools, e-commerce platforms, and ERP systems. This improves operating efficiency and decreases the need for manual data entry.

CRMs have evolved into comprehensive platforms that allow companies to provide more efficient, consistent, and customized customer experiences.

4.2 Essential CRM Functionalities for Companies

With so many CRM solutions at their disposal, companies need to assess platforms according to characteristics that meet their goals and requirements. The following features are thought to be crucial for contemporary CRMs:

Social Media Inclusion:

One of the most important platforms for engaging customers is social media. CRMs that incorporate social media networks enable companies to:

- Track sentiment and brand mentions.

- Answer client questions straight from the CRM interface.
- Monitor engagement and campaign performance indicators.

Automated Task Management and Reminders:

Sales and support teams can better manage follow-ups, contract renewals, and cross-selling possibilities by using automated reminders. This guarantees prompt measures that raise sales closing rates and customer satisfaction.

Insights from AI and Predictive Analytics:

- Predictive analytics uses past data to predict how customers will behave in the future. Identifying clients who are at danger of churn is one example.
- Predicting product preferences in order to suggest tailored deals.
- Emphasizing high-value leads for focused marketing campaigns.

Reports and Dashboards That Can Be Customized:

Teams may quickly access pertinent KPIs and insights with customized dashboards. Businesses may assess campaign

ROI, examine trends, and improve tactics with the use of custom reports.

Accessibility on Mobile Devices:
Mobile-friendly CRMs guarantee that crucial data and features are available anywhere, at any time, since sales and customer support staff frequently operate on the go.

Chatbots and Virtual Assistants Driven by AI:
Real-time customer query response is made possible by integrating AI into CRMs. Additionally, virtual assistants can help users with CRM chores, increasing user productivity and adoption.

By choosing a CRM with these qualities, companies may stay flexible and competitive in a market that is becoming more and more focused on the needs of its customers.

4.3 The Future of CRM Technology Proactive

decision-making, deeper personalization, and smarter automation characterize the future of CRM technology. CRM capabilities will be redefined by emerging technologies like machine learning and artificial intelligence (AI).

The following are important trends influencing CRM's future:

Emotional insights and sentiment analysis:

- CRMs powered by AI are able to evaluate consumer sentiment via voice, text, and social media interactions. For example, identifying a customer's email tone of displeasure and marking it for priority service.
- Finding positive emotion to target happy clients for possibilities to upsell.

Automated and Proactive Decision-Making:

- AI will be used by CRMs in the future to suggest activities based on customer data. Providing discounts or incentives automatically to reduce attrition is one example.
- The best times to follow up are suggested based on trends of consumer activity.

Voice-activated CRM features include:

- Users will be able to use CRM features hands-free thanks to voice assistants. Sales representatives could organize activities during meetings, log updates, and get client data via voice commands.

Experiences That Are Hyper-Personalized:

- Businesses will be able to customize customer experiences in real time with future CRMs. For instance, AI systems may dynamically modify website content according to the preferences of a repeat visitor.
- Customized product packages and prices based on the unique needs of each client.

The use of blockchain technology to improve security

- Integrating blockchain technology into CRMs could provide safe, unchangeable records of client interactions and transactions as data privacy concerns develop.

Integration with the Internet of Things (IoT):

- IoT-enabled CRMs will link to wearables, smart

home appliances, and linked automobiles to gain a better understanding of consumer behavior. For example, a fitness company might suggest health services or goods based on IoT data from wearables.

CRMs will become strategic assets for promoting innovation and expansion as well as tools for managing connections as a result of these developments.

Systems for managing customer relationships are changing dramatically, moving from static databases to sophisticated, all-inclusive platforms. Businesses can use CRMs to strengthen customer connections, increase productivity, and maintain an advantage in a cutthroat market by adopting comprehensive features, incorporating cutting-edge technologies, and predicting future trends. The emergence of intelligent CRMs signals the beginning of a new era in customer engagement, one that is characterized by proactive tactics and data-driven insights.

CHAPTER 5

THE TRANSITION TO MOBILE-FRIENDLY SALES TOOLS

The quick uptake of mobile technology has changed how companies interact with customers and make sales. Having mobile-friendly tools and techniques is now necessary to succeed in the cutthroat industry of today. This chapter examines the function of specialized mobile apps, the growing significance of mobile optimization, and new developments in mobile commerce.

5.1 The Value of Optimizing for Mobile

76% of adults use mobile devices to make purchases, according to current figures. This trend emphasizes how important it is for companies to design mobile experiences that are smooth, responsive, and easy to use.

The Importance of Mobile Optimization:

Modifying Customer Behavior:

These days, mobile devices are the main means of product browsing, research, and purchase. Customers anticipate simple checkout procedures, fast load times, and intuitive navigation. High bounce rates and missed sales chances can result from a sluggish or badly designed mobile experience.

The ranking of search engines:

In their ranking algorithms, search engines such as Google give preference to websites that are optimized for mobile devices. As a result, companies without optimized websites run the risk of losing their place in search results, which will have an immediate effect on traffic and sales.

Increased Accessibility:

Mobile-friendly platforms let companies connect with customers wherever they are at any time. Accessibility boosts engagement and conversions, whether via mobile apps or websites.

The following are the best practices for mobile optimization:

- Make sure the design is responsive, meaning it will adapt to various screen sizes with ease.

- Reduce superfluous scripts and compress pictures to improve page load times.

- Make user interfaces that are easy to use, touch-friendly, and have buttons that are simple to click and navigate.

- Features like autofill and mobile wallet integration (such as Apple Pay and Google Pay) can streamline checkout procedures.

Businesses can remain competitive and relevant in a digital-first environment by giving mobile optimization first priority.

5.2 Creating Sales-Oriented Mobile Apps

A direct and customized way to interact with consumers, foster brand loyalty, and increase sales is through mobile apps. A well-designed mobile application becomes a strategic asset rather than just a useful tool.

Mobile Apps' Advantages for Sales:

Direct Communication:

Real-time updates on sales, restocks, and customized offers are made possible with push notifications. For instance, a fashion retailer can alert app users to special discounts or flash sales.

Improved Customer Experience:

Apps offer a simplified experience, enabling customers to simply browse, purchase, and track orders. Additionally, a lot of applications incorporate reward schemes to promote recurring purchases.

Data Collection and Personalization:

Apps gather important user information, including browsing history, preferences, and past purchases. Businesses are able to increase client satisfaction and provide highly targeted suggestions as a result.

The following are some strategies for developing captivating mobile applications:

- **User-Centric Design:** Give usability and visual appeal first priority. In addition to being visually appealing and consistent with your brand identity, the interface should be easy to use.

- To give customers and teams a cohesive experience, make sure the app seamlessly interacts with your CRM, inventory management, and analytics platforms.

- **Gamification Features:** To improve user engagement and retention, include components like challenges, incentives, or tier-based loyalty programs.

- Consistently enhance the functionality of the app by incorporating the most recent technology developments and responding to customer input.

Creating a mobile application that is suited to the requirements of your target market can greatly boost sales and client loyalty.

5.3 Trends in Mobile Commerce

M-commerce, or mobile commerce, is still developing and changing how customers engage with companies and shop. The enormous potential of mobile platforms to completely transform the retail experience is demonstrated by emerging trends.

The following are the main trends in mobile commerce:

Augmented Reality (AR) Shopping Experiences:
Before making a purchase, shoppers can use AR to see products in their surroundings. Examples include:
- Furniture companies that let consumers use the camera on their smartphones to virtually arrange furniture in their living rooms.
- Cosmetic companies provide virtual makeup product try-ons.

Single-Click Acquisitions:
One-click purchases and other streamlined checkout procedures lower friction and increase conversion rates. This works especially well for impulsive purchases.

The voice of commerce:

With the help of voice assistants like Google Assistant, Alexa, and Siri, customers can now look for and buy things hands-free. To take advantage of this expanding trend, businesses should optimize their mobile platforms for voice search.

PWAs (Progressive Web Apps):

PWAs provide app-like experiences without the need for downloads by fusing the usefulness of mobile apps with the usability of web browsers. They are very responsive, work offline, and load rapidly.

The social commerce sector:

Shopping services are becoming more and more integrated into social networking networks. Examples include the ability for consumers to shop straight from posts and videos on Instagram and TikTok.

- Brands are using "Buy Now" buttons in social media advertisements to make quick transactions.

Adoption of Mobile Wallets:

Due to their safe and easy payment methods, digital wallets like PayPal, Venmo, and Apple Pay are becoming more and more well-liked. Companies that use these strategies see an increase in consumer satisfaction and quicker checkout times.

Prospects for Mobile Commerce in the Future: AI and machine learning will propel even more customization in online buying.

- Blockchain technology has the potential to improve transaction security and transparency.
- Richer, quicker mobile experiences, such as engaging AR/VR shopping, will be made possible by 5G networks.

Businesses may use mobile commerce as a potent growth and innovation engine by staying ahead of these trends.

More than merely a technical tweak, the move to mobile-friendly sales tools signifies a fundamental shift in customer behavior and corporate strategy. Businesses may build lasting relationships with their clients and promote steady growth by putting a high priority on mobile optimization, creating interesting apps, and adopting the newest m-commerce trends. Adaptability and creativity are essential for success in a world that prioritizes mobile devices.

CHAPTER 6

ONLINE PRODUCT SHOWCASES

The emergence of virtual product demos has completely changed how companies showcase their products to potential clients. Virtual demos combine convenience, data-driven insights, and interaction to make them indispensable for contemporary sales tactics. This chapter explores the value of demos, how to include them into marketing initiatives, and how analytics may maximize their effectiveness.

6.1 The Value of Sales Demos

In order to bridge the gap between a customer's interest and their willingness to buy, product demos have long been an essential part of the sales process. This conventional approach is brought into the digital era by virtual demos, which increase their impact, accessibility, and engagement.

The Significance of Virtual Demos:

Promotion of Product Value:

Customers can experience a product's features and advantages in real time during demos. For instance:

- Screen-sharing technology may be used by a SaaS provider to showcase the main features and user interface of a platform.
- Augmented reality (AR) is a tool that furniture retailers may use to let customers see how a couch might appear in their living area.

Building Confidence: Virtual demos reduce hesitancy and foster trust by addressing customer pain areas and showcasing solutions.

- When customers realize how a product fits their unique needs, they are more likely to convert.

By removing geographical restrictions, virtual demos allow companies to showcase their products to a worldwide audience without requiring in-person meetings or travel.

The following are the main benefits of virtual demos over

traditional ones:

Reductions in venue and travel costs.

- Live or recorded sessions provide instant access to a larger audience.
- The ability to quickly and easily customize demos for various client segments.

Businesses can reduce sales cycles and enhance their client acquisition process by giving priority to virtual demonstrations.

6.2 Including Demo Platforms in Advertising Initiatives

Virtual demos are effective resources for marketing initiatives and are not only used as sales tools. They are perfect for generating interest and nurturing leads because of their capacity to inform, educate, and engage.

The following are some tips for using demos in marketing campaigns:

Lead Generation:

Advertise demonstrations as gated material, where users must provide their contact details to gain access. This strategy highlights the potential of your product while producing qualified leads.

Education of Customers:

Include demos in webinars, landing pages, and email marketing campaigns. For example:

- To improve consumer satisfaction after a purchase, an online retailer can produce a video demonstration that shows how to assemble a product.
- Interactive walkthroughs are a useful tool for B2B software companies to introduce clients to sophisticated capabilities and boost adoption rates.

The importance of differentiation

Demos are a great way to highlight the features that make your product unique. Describe how it provides higher value or addresses challenges in a unique way.

Optimal Techniques for Successful Demo Integration:

- Make sure the information is clear and concentrated on the main advantages.

- Make sure the demo fits the target audience and the campaign's messaging.
- Make the lecture real and memorable by using storytelling approaches.

Businesses can enhance their brand messaging and offer prospects value by using virtual demos into marketing campaigns.

6.3 Enhancing Demos using Analytics

Virtual product demos are now dynamic, data-driven experiences instead of static presentations thanks to data analytics. Monitoring user interactions and engagement levels yields information that may be used to improve and streamline the demo procedure.

The following are important metrics to monitor in demo analytics:

Engagement Duration:

Determine the duration of users' engagement with the demo. While drop-off points might draw attention to areas that want work, longer periods show persistent interest.

Hubs for Interaction:

During the demo, keep track of the features or portions that get the greatest attention. Future product development and marketing plans can benefit from these findings.

Rates of Conversion:

Calculate the proportion of demo attendees who move on to the next round of the sales funnel, like setting up a meeting or buying something.

Collecting Feedback:

To get immediate feedback from participants regarding their experience, use ratings or surveys after the demo.

How Data Improves Demo Performance:

Customized Presentations:

Customize demos for particular client segments by using data. For example, a small business showcase may emphasize cost-effectiveness, whereas an enterprise demo might emphasize scalability.

Continuous Improvement:

Iterative improvements are made possible by analytics, which show what works and what doesn't. For instance, you can change or eliminate a certain portion of the demo if analytics reveal that users are often disengaging during it.

Predictive Information:

Sales teams can prioritize high-potential prospects by using AI-powered advanced analytics solutions that can forecast consumer behavior based on demo interactions.

Implementing Analytics in Virtual Demos:

- For uniform data tracking, use technologies that easily interact with your CRM.
- Use click tracking and heatmaps to do a thorough interaction study.
- Plan on reviewing demo performance on a regular basis to make sure it aligns with company objectives.

With analytics, virtual demos transform from a simple presenting tool into a strategic asset that adapts constantly to the needs of the client.

In the current digital sales environment, virtual product presentations are essential. They offer a captivating means of demonstrating value, cultivating client trust, and broadening the audience. Businesses can improve their strategy and achieve greater results by incorporating these tools into marketing campaigns and utilizing data. Learning the art and science of virtual demos is essential for long-term success in a time when the client experience is paramount.

CHAPTER 7

SALES CALL ANALYTICS

Voice communication is still a crucial touchpoint in sales contacts in a world that is becoming more and more digital. Call analytics uses contemporary technology to convert voice data into insights that can be put to use, helping companies improve customer happiness, sales performance, and strategy. The strategic value of call analytics, the use of AI and machine learning to call analysis, and the integration of call analytics with CRM and other tools for a cohesive sales approach are all covered in this chapter.

7.1 Call Analytics' Function in Sales Strategy

The way that companies handle sales and consumer relations has been completely transformed by call analytics. Businesses obtain previously unobtainable insights by examining speech interactions, giving them a major competitive advantage in marketplaces.

The following are the main purposes of call analytics in sales:

Comprehending customer intent:

Tools for call analytics can pinpoint the precise requirements and problems of clients. Businesses can ascertain why customers are contacting them by identifying phrases and patterns during calls.

- What remedies they are looking for.
- How to effectively adjust answers to meet their needs.

Evaluating Customer Contentment:

consumer satisfaction levels can be inferred using metrics such as sentiment detection and tone analysis, which assist in assessing consumer emotions during interactions. For instance:

- A successful resolution may be indicated by positive tone alterations.
- Recurring complaints or negative tone could indicate unsolved problems.

Assessing the Quality of Leads:

Leads are not all made equal. By examining a lead's degree of involvement, queries, and urgency during the contact, call analytics assesses the lead's prospective worth.

The following are some advantages of using call analytics to shape sales strategy:

- By classifying leads according to the quality of their interactions, it enhances consumer segmentation.
- By recognizing common consumer preferences or objections, it aids in improving sales pitches.
- By identifying the areas in which salespeople require development, it provides training opportunities.

Businesses can better match their sales approach with consumer expectations and get greater results by integrating call analytics into their strategy.

7.2 Call Analysis Using AI and Machine Learning

Call analytics has advanced from basic data gathering to

predictive and prescriptive insights because to the combination of artificial intelligence (AI) and machine learning (ML). These technologies give sales teams strong decision-making tools by swiftly and accurately analyzing large volumes of call data.

The transformation of call analytics using AI and machine learning:

Speech-to-Text Transcription:
Spoken language is transformed into text by AI-powered systems, which facilitates conversation analysis for sentiments, patterns, and keywords.

- For example, terms like "price" or "discount" may result in automated replies or follow-up flags.

In order to interpret emotional states, machine learning algorithms evaluate vocal inflections, pitch, and tempo. Sales teams can use this information to:

- Recognize when a customer is unhappy and requires further assistance.
- Acknowledge zeal, as it could signify a desire to seal a transaction.

Recognizing Trends and Patterns:

Businesses can modify their strategy by using AI to find common phrases, reoccurring issues, and behavioral patterns over numerous calls.

AI in Call Analytics Applications Examples:

- **Real-Time Coaching:** AI gives sales agents real-time feedback during calls, recommending improved wording or providing speedy information retrieval.
- **Predictive Analytics:** AI forecasts the chance of conversion or churn based on current call dynamics by examining past data.
- **Automation of Quality Assurance:** AI evaluates interactions for compliance, efficacy, and script adherence in place of human analyzing calls.

The following are some benefits of using AI and ML in call analytics:

- **Scalability:** AI effectively manages massive data sets.

- **Precision:** As machine learning algorithms advance, they provide insights that are more and more accurate.
- **Proactivity:** Businesses may anticipate and respond to client needs with the aid of predictive capabilities.

Call analytics is transformed from a reactive tool into a proactive driver of sales performance by utilizing AI and machine learning.

7.3 Connecting CRM and Other Tools with Call Analytics

Call analytics must be easily connected with CRM systems and other sales tools in order to provide the most value. Effective data flow between platforms is ensured by this integration, facilitating strategic and cohesive decision-making.

Advantages of Integration:

Detailed Client Profiles:

CRM platforms and call analytics data sync to give

organizations a comprehensive picture of their clients.

- This comprises sentiment analysis and call history.
- Purchase preferences and history.
- Insights from continuous encounters in real time.

Simplified Follow-Ups:

Sales teams can automate follow-ups based on call outcomes thanks to integration. An automated thank-you email could be triggered, for instance, by positive sentiment during a call.

- If concerns are voiced, a follow-up conversation with a senior representative may be scheduled.

Better Interaction Between Teams:

To provide a cohesive approach to customer interaction, marketing, product development, and customer care teams can utilize call analytics insights contained in CRM systems.

1. The first step in integrating call analytics with CRM is to select compatible tools. Choose call analytics products that have strong APIs or native CRM connectivity.

2. **Customize Data Mapping:** In your CRM, specify how call analytics data (such as sentiment ratings, keywords, and call duration) will be shown.

3. **Workflow Trigger Automation:** Workflows like assigning leads, sending follow-up emails, or flagging concerns for escalation can be started using analytics data.

4. **Train Teams on Usage:** Make sure managers and salespeople know how to access and utilize the integrated data efficiently.

Connecting with Additional Tools:

Marketing Platforms:

- Call analytics can be synchronized with marketing tools to assist in campaign refinement based on customer feedback obtained during calls.

- **Sales Enablement Tools:** Call analytics data can help create training materials and sales scripts that are more successful.

- **Systems for Customer Support:** Consistent and sympathetic replies across channels are ensured by sharing call insights with support personnel.

Businesses may establish a smooth ecosystem that facilitates data-driven decision-making and customer-centric initiatives by integrating call analytics with CRM and other systems.

Call analytics, which provide deep insights into customer behavior and preferences, have emerged as a key component of contemporary sales methods. Businesses may improve sales pitches, find hidden trends, and make remarkably accurate consumer requirements predictions with the use of AI and machine learning. By combining these features with CRM systems, insights are guaranteed to be actionable and team-aligned. Understanding call analytics is essential for sales success in today's data-driven environment, as voice interactions continue to be a critical component of client engagement.

CHAPTER 8

TRENDS IN TECHNOLOGY INVESTMENT

Technology is becoming a vital instrument for increasing productivity, comprehending consumer behavior, and spurring growth in the quickly changing field of sales. However, careful investment techniques are necessary for effective adoption. In order to stay ahead of the competition in a cutthroat market, this chapter examines how companies should maximize their technological expenditures, weigh cost against value, and predict emerging trends.

8.1 Strategic Investment in Technology

Investing strategically in sales technology entails giving top priority to instruments that meet long-term corporate objectives and provide quantifiable value. By making sure their technological ecosystem supports scalability and operational efficiency, firms may optimize return on investment (ROI) from developments in CRMs, scheduling platforms, and customer analytics tools.

The following are the main areas where strategic technology investment is needed:

1. CRM (customer relationship management) systems:

- CRMs are essential for tracking interactions, storing customer data, and facilitating targeted marketing campaigns.
- In order to ensure that sales teams concentrate on high-potential leads, advanced CRMs incorporate AI for predictive analytics.
- Salesforce, HubSpot, and Zoho CRM are a few examples.

2. Scheduling and Automation Tools:

- By lowering administrative burdens, such as email follow-ups and automatic schedulers, sales teams can focus on developing relationships.
- Calendly for meeting scheduling and Zapier for app-to-app workflow automation are two examples.

3. consumer Analytics Platforms:

- Analytics solutions are essential for improving sales strategies since they help firms analyze consumer behavior, preferences, and trends.
- Tableau and Google Analytics are two examples.

4. Sales Enablement Tools:

- These comprise AI-powered coaching tools, training platforms, and content management systems to give teams the tools they need to succeed.
- Highspot and seismic are two examples.

Strategic Technology Spending Has the Following Advantages:

- Automating repetitive processes improves operational efficiency.
- Improved insights and customisation lead to higher levels of consumer satisfaction.
- Enhances the sales and marketing teams' alignment, resulting in a smooth customer experience.

Businesses must match technology investments with their overarching strategy in order to optimize returns, making sure that they meet current demands while maintaining flexibility for expansion in the future.

8.2 Keeping Value and Cost in Check

Determining which tools are worth the investment is a challenge brought on by the expanding variety of sales technologies. To guarantee that resources are distributed efficiently without sacrificing innovation, cost and value must be balanced.

The following are important factors to take into account when evaluating cost and value:

Initial Cost vs. Long-Term Savings:
- Some technologies may be expensive up front, but they might save a lot of money over time by increasing productivity or lowering customer attrition.
- For instance, while AI-driven solutions may necessitate a significant financial outlay, they might increase conversion rates and streamline procedures, providing long-term benefits.

Scalability:

- Select tools that will expand with your company. A higher return on investment is guaranteed by a platform that facilitates market development or the onboarding of larger teams.
- As an illustration, cloud-based solutions frequently offer scalable alternatives at a lesser cost than on-premise systems.

Integration Capabilities:

- Assess how well the technology works with your current systems. Ineffective integration might result in extra expenses and inefficiencies.
- For instance, CRMs that integrate with analytics software and marketing automation platforms lessen data silos.

User Adoption:

- The effectiveness of technology's utilization determines its value. To guarantee acceptance, make an investment in tools that are easy to use and offer sufficient training.

Cost-Effectiveness Strategies:

- Before investing in new technology, perform ROI evaluations to estimate possible advantages.
- Before implementing the technologies throughout the entire organization, test their effectiveness with small teams.
- Make use of Software as a Service (SaaS) options that enable upgrades and flexible payment schedules.

Carefully weighing the long-term advantages and short-term costs is necessary to strike a balance between cost and value. Sustainable investment plans are ensured by giving priority to technologies that provide quantifiable results.

8.3 Prospects for Investments in Sales Technology

Businesses must foresee and adjust to new trends as technology develops further in order to stay competitive. The sales landscape is changing as a result of advancements in blockchain, augmented reality, and virtual reality. These technologies present chances for increased client interaction and operational efficiency.

Important Prospects for Future Investment:

1. Virtual reality (VR) and augmented reality (AR):

- **AR in Product Demonstrations**: AR enhances the purchasing experience by enabling buyers to see products in real-world environments.
- For instance, home décor businesses let their clients virtually arrange furniture in their spaces.
- **VR for Immersive Sales Experiences:** VR produces immersive settings for training sessions or product demonstrations.
- An example would be a virtual reality demonstration of a luxury car that lets buyers interact with its features.

2. Machine learning (ML) and artificial intelligence (AI):

- AI will keep spurring advancements in real-time decision-making tools, conversational AI, and predictive analytics.
- Lead scoring will be improved by ML models,

which will assist sales teams in concentrating on high-value prospects.

3. Blockchain for Transparent Transactions:

- Blockchain technology can improve trust in digital transactions, provide transparent pricing, and simplify contracts.
- Smart contracts, for instance, can automate terms of payment in business-to-business transactions.

In order to provide hyper-individualized marketing campaigns and customer experiences, future solutions will leverage big data and artificial intelligence.

E-commerce sites that provide dynamic pricing according to consumer behavior and industry trends are one example.

5. Voice-Activated Sales Tools: Voice technology will play a crucial role in sales procedures by facilitating customer communication, CRM navigation, and hands-free data entry.

- Voice assistants with AI capabilities, for instance, can analyze and react to sales queries instantly.

Getting Ready for Future Trends:

- Fund trial projects to test new technologies without spending too much money.
- Attend tech-focused conferences or workshops and keep up with industry advancements.
- Form alliances with tech companies to obtain competitive insights and access state-of-the-art solutions.

Adopting technologies that promote innovation, enhance client relationships, and streamline operations is where sales technology expenditures are headed. Companies will establish themselves as leaders in their sectors if they respond swiftly to these developments.

Sales technology investment necessitates a strategic approach that strikes a balance between short-term demands and long-term objectives. Businesses can boost customer satisfaction and promote growth by concentrating on technologies that provide quantifiable value, evaluating cost-effectiveness, and staying ahead of developing trends. Businesses now have great chances to lead and innovate in the changing sales landscape as a result of the transition towards AR, VR, blockchain, and AI. Sales teams can use technology to achieve long-term success with careful planning and proactive adoption.

CHAPTER 9

Capitalizing on New Sales Patterns

The sales environment is always changing due to societal goals, changing consumer expectations, and technological breakthroughs. Companies can gain a competitive edge and satisfy client requests by adjusting to these new trends. This chapter examines the ways in which sustainability-focused technologies, conversational commerce, and customized sales journeys are revolutionizing customer interaction and sales tactics.

9.1 Talkative Business

The term "conversational commerce" describes the use of AI-powered technologies, including chatbots and virtual assistants, to enable smooth, instantaneous communication between companies and clients. By facilitating individualized communication, enhancing client engagement, and expediting transactions, this trend is revolutionizing the sales process.

The following are the main characteristics of conversational commerce:

1. 24/7 Availability:

- Chatbots and AI assistants are available 24/7, guaranteeing that clients receive prompt assistance regardless of time zones.
- An example might be a chatbot on an online store helping consumers with late-night product questions.

2. Seamless Purchasing Experiences:

- Conversational tools make purchasing easier by recommending products, responding to inquiries, and even completing transactions all within the chat window.
- An illustration would be a consumer employing a virtual assistant to browse a retailer's website, select the appropriate size, and place an order straight away.

3. Data-Driven Personalization:

- AI systems examine user activity to provide customized recommendations and foresee client requirements.

- An illustration might be a chatbot that suggests accessories based on a customer's most recent purchases.

Business Benefits:

1. **Higher Conversion Rates:** Providing real-time support guarantees a more seamless checkout process and lowers cart abandonment.

2. **Improved Customer Satisfaction:** Accurate and prompt responses improve the client experience in general.

3. **Scalability:** Conversational solutions enable companies to manage high client query volumes without needing a substantial increase in staff.

Incorporating voice assistants, natural language processing (NLP), and omnichannel capabilities will increase the efficacy of conversational commerce as it develops further.

9.2 Tailored Sales Experiences

Consumers of today need experiences that are customized to meet their own requirements and tastes. Businesses may create customized sales experiences that increase repeat business, develop loyalty, and establish trust by utilizing data and artificial intelligence.

1. The first component of a personalized sales journey is customer segmentation. By breaking down clients into focused groups according to their demographics, activity, and past purchases, marketing campaigns can be more successfully executed.

- An illustration would be a clothes retailer developing advertising campaigns for "seasonal buyers" and "frequent shoppers."

2. Dynamic Content Delivery:

- Relevance is guaranteed by using AI-driven technologies to deliver tailored content, like product recommendations or targeted advertisements.
- An illustration would be streaming services that

suggest shows to users depending on their viewing preferences.

Predictive Analytics for Anticipation:

- By examining patterns, AI may forecast future customer requirements, enabling companies to offer solutions before the client even recognizes their need.
- An illustration would be a subscription service that offers renewals or refills when it notices that a product may be running low.

The following are some advantages of personalization:

- Better Customer Relationships: Personalized interactions increase trust and provide customers a sense of value.
- **Increased Sales:** Customized suggestions match client preferences, increasing the possibility that a transaction will be made.
- **Increased Brand Loyalty**: Consumers are more likely to patronize companies that cater to their individual demands.

Implementation Strategies:

- To consolidate customer data and facilitate personalization, invest in strong CRM systems.
- Sales personnel should receive training on how to analyze data insights and make tailored proposals.
- Make use of marketing automation solutions to send customized messages via social media, email, and other platforms.

The secret to success is striking a balance between privacy and personalization while making sure that data gathering and use follow legal and ethical requirements.

9.3 Technology and Sustainability in Sales

Consumers are increasingly considering sustainability while making decisions, giving preference to companies that exhibit social and environmental responsibility. Technology is a key factor in coordinating sales tactics with sustainability objectives, opening up new avenues for attracting eco-conscious customers.

How Sustainability Influences Sales:

1. Eco-Friendly Products:

- Offering sustainable product options, such as those created from recycled materials, appeals to environmentally aware shoppers.
- An illustration might be a cosmetics company advertising its reusable containers.

2. Transparency in Supply Chains:

- Businesses may give clients a comprehensive picture of the path taken by their products, from sourcing to delivery, by utilizing blockchain technology.
- An example would be a coffee company that uses a QR code to let customers track the provenance of their coffee beans.

3. Digital Sales Channels:

- Making the switch to digital platforms lessens the environmental effect of printed goods and physical storefronts.
- For instance, online product catalogs are taking the place of conventional print brochures.

Technological Advancements Fueling Sustainability:

- **Carbon Footprint Calculators:** Resources that assist companies and customers in comprehending how their purchases affect the environment.
- **AI for Inventory Management:** AI reduces waste and overproduction by optimizing inventory levels.
- Green logistics refers to technologies that optimize delivery routes in order to minimize fuel usage and emissions.

The following are some advantages of sustainable sales practices:

- **Enhanced Brand Reputation:** Businesses that put sustainability first win over customers and set themselves apart from rivals.
- **Cost Savings:** Operating costs are decreased by cutting waste and making the most of resources.
- **Bringing in New Audiences:** Younger generations are more receptive to eco-friendly efforts and are inclined to support sustainable products.

Implementation Strategies:
- Make an operational investment in renewable energy

solutions.

- Collaborate with environmentally conscious vendors and highlight sustainability in advertising initiatives.
- Constantly assess and enhance environmental practices using insights from technology.

Sustainability in sales is now a competitive need rather than an option. Businesses that adopt this trend and use cutting-edge technologies will improve their market position in addition to making the world a healthier place.

Businesses hoping to remain relevant in a market that is changing quickly must take advantage of new sales trends. While personalized sales tactics create enduring relationships through customized experiences, conversational commerce provides real-time, AI-powered engagement that expedites the customer journey. In the meanwhile, companies can match with contemporary consumer values and cultivate customer loyalty among environmentally conscious consumers by implementing sustainability-driven technologies.

Businesses can establish themselves as leaders in

innovation, consumer happiness, and ethical responsibility by comprehending and implementing these trends. Those who successfully integrate technology, personalization, and sustainability to provide meaningful, value-driven experiences will be the ones who succeed in this new sales era.

CHAPTER 10

USING TECHNOLOGY TO STAY AHEAD IN SALES

To stay competitive at a time when technology is always evolving, companies need to proactively incorporate new developments into their sales strategies. Maintaining technological leadership requires alertness, flexibility, and a dedication to providing teams with the resources and know-how they need to succeed. In order to achieve long-term success, this chapter explores the significance of keeping an eye on trends, remaining adaptable, and developing a tech-savvy sales staff.

10.1 Following the Trends

There are advantages and disadvantages to the quick speed of technical advancement in sales. Companies that keep a close eye on advancements can use state-of-the-art solutions to improve customer relations, streamline operations, and obtain a competitive advantage.

1. The first step in staying current is to regularly read industry publications, whitepapers, and case studies to gain insight into new technologies and tactics.

- An illustration would be a sales team leader who follows CRM developments by subscribing to Gartner reports.

2. Networking and Conferences:

- To gain knowledge from peers and professionals, participate in webinars, sales technology expos, and networking events.
- For instance, attending conferences such as Salesforce Dreamforce to learn about cutting-edge technology and industry best practices.

3. Technological Provider Collaborations:

- Collaborate with technology providers to gain early access to new features and insights on upcoming advancements.
- As an illustration, consider beta testing a new AI-powered lead scoring program.

The Advantages of Trend Awareness:

- **First-Mover Advantage:** Businesses can differentiate themselves from rivals by embracing innovative technologies early.

- **Improving Customer Experiences:** Staying up to date with trends guarantees that customers' expectations are fulfilled or surpassed.

- **Informed Decision-Making:** Companies can make calculated investments in instruments that support their objectives.

A culture of continuous learning is necessary to be future-focused, where teams are receptive to innovation and continue to be curious about new developments.

10.2 Developing an Adaptable Mentality

Success in modern sales is largely dependent on technological adaptation. To remain relevant in a fast changing environment, businesses must be prepared to change course and welcome change.

The following are important components of flexibility:

1. Rapid Technology Adoption:

- Rapidly assess and incorporate new technologies without interfering with business operations.
- Using virtual reality (VR) platforms for engaging product demos is one example.

2. Scalable Infrastructure:

- Invest in modular and cloud-based solutions that can expand with your company.
- For instance, moving CRM systems to the cloud to enable smooth scalability.

3. Feedback loops and experimentation:

- Pilot new technologies and collect team input to improve implementation tactics.
- Before a wide launch, AI-powered chatbots might be tested on a smaller sample of consumers.

Why Flexibility Is Important:

- **Adapting to Market Shifts:** Businesses may react to shifting consumer demands and market conditions by adopting a flexible strategy.
- **Seizing Opportunities:** Businesses can take

advantage of new trends before their rivals can by implementing new tools quickly.

- Experimentation reduces the risk of making significant investments in unproven technology.

Businesses must develop a culture that values agility, promotes innovation, and sees obstacles as chances for development if they want to promote flexibility.

10.3 Developing a Tech-Aware Sales Force

The people who use the technology determine its success, regardless of how sophisticated it is. To maximize ROI and boost performance, sales teams must be prepared with the know-how to use cutting-edge solutions.

How to Assemble a Tech-Aware Sales Staff:

1. All-inclusive Training Programs:

- Offer practical instruction to acquaint teams with new features and technologies.
- For instance, setting up CRM analytics seminars to equip salespeople with insights based on data.

2. Continuous Upskilling:

- Promote lifelong learning with workshops, online courses, and certificates.
- One example might be enrolling team members in a sales AI training on LinkedIn Learning.

3. Cross-Functional Collaboration:

- Encourage cooperation amongst marketing, IT, and sales teams to guarantee seamless technology integration.
- To guarantee user-centric implementation, for instance, sales teams should be involved early in the process of choosing a new sales platform.

4. Gamification and Incentives:

- To make tech adoption interesting, use gamified learning materials and incentive schemes.
- Acknowledging high achievers who successfully integrate new tools into their processes is one example.

A Tech-Savvy Team's Advantages:

- **More Productivity:** Teams that become proficient with cutting-edge tools are able to automate repetitive chores and concentrate on strategic endeavors.
- Better Decision-Making: Competent staff members are able to evaluate and decipher data to derive useful insights.
- **Increased Morale:** Equipping teams with technology boosts self-esteem and contentment at work.

The following are important technologies that sales teams should become proficient in:

- **CRM Platforms:** for monitoring sales activity and maintaining client connections.
- **Analytics Tools:** To analyze information and spot patterns.
- **AI Assistants:** To enhance lead generation and automate tedious chores.

The purpose of mobile sales apps is to guarantee productivity while on the go.

Businesses may turn their sales people into tech-savvy professionals who can use technology to get the best outcomes by placing a high priority on education and engagement.

Keeping up with technological advancements in sales is a continuous process that calls for empowerment, awareness, and flexibility. Companies need to keep a close eye on trends in order to stay up to date on developments and be ready to change course as necessary. A well-trained, tech-savvy sales crew guarantees that these technologies are utilized to their fullest capacity, while a flexible mentality facilitates the smooth integration of new tools.

Businesses who place a high priority on technology innovation and provide their employees with the tools they need to fully utilize its potential will not only remain competitive in this quickly changing market, but they will also redefine what it means to be a successful salesperson. Companies can establish themselves as leaders in the contemporary sales environment by fusing strategic vision, flexibility, and human capital investment.

ABOUT THE AUTHOR

 Author and thought leader in the IT field Taylor Royce is well known. He has a two-decade career and is an expert at tech trend analysis and forecasting, which enables a wide audience to understand complicated concepts.

Royce's considerable involvement in the IT industry stemmed from his passion with technology, which he developed during his computer science studies. He has extensive knowledge of the industry because of his experience in both software development and strategic consulting.

Known for his research and lucidity, he has written multiple best-selling books and contributed to esteemed tech periodicals. Translations of Royce's books throughout the world demonstrate his impact.

Royce is a well-known authority on emerging technologies and their effects on society, frequently requested as a speaker at international conferences and as a guest on tech podcasts. He promotes the development of ethical technology, emphasizing problems like data privacy and the digital divide.

In addition, with a focus on sustainable industry growth, Royce mentors upcoming tech experts and supports IT education projects. Taylor Royce is well known for his ability to combine analytical thinking with technical know-how. He sees a time when technology will ethically benefit humanity.

www.ingramcontent.com/pod-product-compliance
Lightning Source LLC
Chambersburg PA
CBHW070112230526
45472CB00004B/1228